JOURNEY
to
HEALTH

Journey to Health

By
Heather Michael

XULON PRESS

Xulon Press
2301 Lucien Way #415
Maitland, FL 32751
407.339.4217
www.xulonpress.com

© 2021 by Heather Michael

All rights reserved solely by the author. The author guarantees all contents are original and do not infringe upon the legal rights of any other person or work. No part of this book may be reproduced in any form without the permission of the author. The views expressed in this book are not necessarily those of the publisher.

Due to the changing nature of the Internet, if there are any web addresses, links, or URLs included in this manuscript, these may have been altered and may no longer be accessible. The views and opinions shared in this book belong solely to the author and do not necessarily reflect those of the publisher. The publisher therefore disclaims responsibility for the views or opinions expressed within the work.

Unless otherwise indicated, Scripture quotations taken from the Holy Bible, New International Version (NIV). Copyright © 1973, 1978, 1984, 2011 by Biblica, Inc.™. Used by permission. All rights reserved.

Printed in the United States of America.

Paperback ISBN-13: 978-1-6628-1431-0
eBook ISBN-13: 978-1-6628-1432-7

The Lord is faithful to his promises and loving towards all He has made.

(Psalm 145:13)

Table of Contents

Acknowledgements viii
Introduction. xi

Chapter 1	The Beginning of the Story.	1
Chapter 2	The Beginning of the Journey.	9
Chapter 3	Food Intolerances	13
Chapter 4	The Journey Continues…	19
Chapter 5	Back to the Beginning?	29
Chapter 6	Glyphosate	33
Chapter 7	Organic vs Non-Organic.	37
Chapter 8	How Wheat Has Changed…	39
Chapter 9	2020 Dirty Dozen Foods.	43
Chapter 10	2020 Clean Fifteen Foods	45
Chapter 11	A2 Milk.	53
Chapter 12	E Numbers.	57
Chapter 13	Digestive Enzymes.	63
Chapter 14	Recipes.	65
Chapter 15	Yogurt Making	97
Chapter 16	Ice Cream!	99
Chapter 17	Products.	103

Conclusion 105
Bibliography. 107

Acknowledgements

Thanks to my parents, who have supported us on our journey from the beginning and lent a listening ear when times were challenging.

Thanks to my mother-in-law, Audrey, who has faithfully prayed for Rebekah.

Also thanks to my husband, Allister, and my children, Rachael, Rebekah, and Caleb, for their patience and support throughout the time it took to write this book

I want to give my appreciation to Darren Allen, our local pharmacist, who has a wealth of knowledge in this field. He has guided me over the past three years and patiently answered numerous questions. I value the help he has given in diagnosing Rebekah's intolerance.

Thanks to the doctors and consultants who have all had a valuable role to play in our journey.

And of course, thanks to friends who have prayed. Knowing that others have taken the time to care for and pray for Rebekah through the struggles she has faced has meant so much. I particularly want to mention the members of the "Prayers for Parliament" (PfP) group, who have prayed so faithfully for Rebekah throughout a very trying time.

I appreciate the advice from my friend, Libby, who has listened patiently and spoken to me from her own experience. And to all those who have supported me on the journey to writing this book: Thank you!

But I cannot conclude this section without thanking the Lord—the One who has guided us and continues to guide us through each step of our journey to health.

Introduction

Every supermarket has an aisle devoted to "Free From" products. This section of the food industry is growing, as are the number of people suffering from food allergies or food intolerances. This could include an allergy/intolerance to wheat, gluten, dairy, or eggs, to name but a few.

What is the cause? Why has there been an increase in allergies and intolerances?

Throughout the course of this book, I will be exploring possible causes for this surge of allergies/intolerances in our society. I will delve into what is hidden in the food we eat and how, as I have heard it said, "we are what we eat."

I will also be sharing our family's journey, which began when my daughter Rebekah (8) developed a food intolerance and digestive problems. This is a journey which continues to this day.

I was inspired to write this book after reading 2 Corinthians 1:3-4, which read:

> *"Praise be to the God and Father of our Lord Jesus Christ, the Father of compassion and the God of all comfort, who comforts us in our troubles, so that we can comfort those in any trouble with the comfort we ourselves have received from God."*

God has helped me every step of the way in this journey. He has never let me down, and has comforted me when it was challenging by guiding me along the right pathways. This could have been finding a new product after an internet search, or fresh insight as a result of a conversation. The Lord also provided many companions along the way who prayed for and supported me, lending listening ears when I needed them.

If you are reading this book, then chances are you may be suffering from a food intolerance or know someone who does.

I hope by reading this book you will develop a better understanding of possible causes of allergies/intolerances and realize that you are not alone in your journey.

I have included some pointers to further research, as well as some tips and recipes I have picked up along the way.

Food intolerances are challenging, I hope to help and encourage you as we navigate this together.

CHAPTER 1

The Beginning of the Story

Although this book was intended to speak of Rebekah's individual journey, I felt it appropriate to include a condensed version of the path which the Lord has led us through as a family as well.

One of my desires in life was to be married and have children. It looked unlikely for so long. My friends were all married with children and there were no eligible men on the horizon. I prayed that God would give me a husband and children. About twenty-five years ago I received two pictures from God, which I kept close to my heart and which gave me hope in the years to come.

The first was a picture of a hand with a wedding ring, which reassured me that I would one day be married, but the second picture was more specific; it showed two children, both with dark hair. The first was a girl and the second a boy, but the girl was significantly taller than the boy. From that picture I believed God was giving me a promise of two children, the first of which would be a girl.

Years passed, but my desire to have a family and children did not. It looked unlikely that either of these things would ever happen on their own, so I thought I could perhaps take action to make at least one thing happen...

I lived in Cookstown, Northern Ireland, but spent the weekends in Coleraine with my parents, who lived an hour away. On Sunday mornings I would drive back to Cookstown, where I was involved in the local Methodist Church. One particular Sunday morning, as I drove to Cookstown, my thoughts were totally preoccupied with children and I began considering the idea of adoption. I went to church to get Sunday School organized, as I was one of the leaders, and I was walking across the church hall when the Lord spoke to me so clearly, it could almost have been an audible voice. "Don't go and get an Ishmael," He said. That stopped me in my tracks!

Let me explain by going back a few thousand years to the biblical story of Abraham.

God had promised Abraham a son. In fact, not only a son, but one that would become the father of a nation! As years passed it looked unlikely Abraham would ever have a child. Abraham was now eighty-six, and his wife Sarah was seventy-seven. They had now been waiting expectantly for eleven years without a hint of the promise being fulfilled. In fact, it looked more unlikely by the day. Instead of continuing to wait, Abraham decided to conceive a child through Sarah's maidservant, Hagar. Hagar gave birth to a son, called Ishamael. But Ishmael was not the child God had promised, and this caused problems. Thirteen years later, however, Sarah (aged ninety) gave birth at last to the child God had promised, who was given the name Isaac. By this stage Abraham was ninety-nine!

I realized that by considering adoption, I was going down a similar route to Abraham, trying to fulfil God's promise by my own means! It says in Genesis:

> *"Abraham believed God and he credited it to him as righteousness." (Genesis 15:6)*

I chose to believe God and trust in Him.

I waited many years. I searched Christian websites online until I met Philip. On our first meeting Philip suggested that his friend Allister would be a better match for me, so on January 5, 2005, I met Allister. Our relationship developed quickly, and we got married on July 7, 2006. We were both thirty-seven. Were we too old for God to fulfil His promise? With God, nothing is impossible.

In September I discovered I was pregnant with my first child. This was short-lived, however, as I miscarried on October 13, 2006, at eight weeks pregnant. This was devastating and left me feeling so empty.

I conceived again and feared I would lose this child too, so I lay in bed and asked many to pray that the child I was carrying would survive. God answered those prayers, and on August 17, 2007, Rachael was born. The pregnancy had been traumatic, so I decided one child was enough, but sometime later God began to stir my heart to desire another child and I knew His total promise had not yet been fulfilled.

By this stage I was moving into a new and difficult season, a season of infertility. I longed for another child, but infertility was now a barrier.

It took time to get pregnant but I eventually did. There was a lot of heartache and frustration, though, as over the course of the following four years I miscarried four babies, each in the early stages of pregnancy. I felt the Lord telling me to prepare my body, so I did some research and took the recommended supplements in addition to prescribed medication to help prevent miscarriage.

In February of 2011 I discovered I was pregnant for the seventh time. As with my previous pregnancies, it was an anxious wait to reach the twelve-week mark.

On April 23, 2011, it was Allister's birthday. It was also the day before Easter Sunday, and we decided to go for a day trip to the zoo with Rachael to celebrate. Rachael was three at that time. That night I began to experience the familiar signs associated with miscarriage. It was late, but I rang my mum, who tried to console me over the phone. I felt I couldn't go through another miscarriage. By that stage I had lost five babies and couldn't cope with losing another one.

I rested over the next few days. God began to show me that there was a difference between believing and having faith. I believed in my *head* that I would have another child, but I needed to have that faith deep down and know that God would give me that child. I saw the verse, "*I believe, help my unbelief*"[1] in a new light. I held tightly to God and He kept my baby safe in my womb.

Given my history, I was scanned monthly. My mum came along with me for the twenty-week scan. I asked the radiologist if it was a boy, as God had shown me a girl and a boy in my picture. I was so taken aback when I was told it was a girl! I even asked if she was sure. Had I misunderstood what God had shown me? I

---

[1] Mark 9 v 24 (KJV)

couldn't fathom what was going on. But on November 10, 2011, Rebekah Sarah was born. I was forty-two! Just as Sarah had to wait twenty-four years for God to fulfil the promise he had made to Abraham, I had waited about eighteen.

> *"I will make you into a great nation."*
> *(Genesis 12:2)*

Rebekah's second name, Sarah, reminds me that God was faithful in my wait, just as He was with Abraham and Sarah.

I realized that God hadn't fulfilled His promise—that a baby boy was yet to come. One day, as I was wheeling Rebekah in the pram, God impressed on my heart that my baby boy, who would one day be born, was to be called Caleb, as he would be a kingdom man. He would be a man who would serve God boldly, as Caleb did in biblical times. And so I held on to the promise and the name. God was still at work. I relayed this to my childminder and she stood with me in faith. She almost felt as if she should write his name down in her books in anticipation!

And so my baby boy was conceived. This was the smoothest pregnancy. Caleb was born on April 11, 2013. I was two months short of being forty-four!

Both Rachael and Caleb had dark hair as the Lord had shown. My surprise in the middle was blond!

Who says God doesn't keep His promises? He is faithful and continues to be faithful.

He has fulfilled His promises and given us the blessing of three precious and wonderful children. Our three miracles. He gave me more than I could have expected

> *"Now to Him who can do immeasurably more than all we can ask or imagine, to Him be glory." (Ephesians 3:20)*

We have seen where God has been leading us; let's now jump to the next stage of the journey, which began in December 2017.

CHAPTER 2

The Beginning of the Journey

None of us had any idea what life would be like with food intolerances. My kids were generally healthy and well until December 2017, when Rebekah (6) and Caleb (4) both developed throat infections. Both had temperatures and both were on antibiotics. Their throat infections were soon clear, but Rebekah, however, began complaining of a sore tummy, which didn't seem to go away.

We tried all the usual advice—hot water bottles, massaging the tummy—but nothing seemed to bring the desired relief. She was checked by doctors but nothing was found. She kept complaining but nothing I did would help. Mornings were worse, as she woke feeling very nauseous and getting out of bed was an ordeal for her. She would refuse breakfast, and on mornings when her tummy was worse than usual, Rebekah would refuse to get dressed, pushing any offers of help away.

It caused her great distress, so on some mornings she came to school late, which gave her time to calm down enough to cope with some breakfast.

At school Rebekah complained to her teacher regularly. I had no idea what was causing the pain and discomfort. On a visit to the GP in January 2018, bacteria was found in her urine. The sample was sent to the lab and a few days later I was contacted by the GP about an unusual strain of bacteria that had shown up. Rebekah was given an antibiotic and her tummy pain improved. As a result of the unusual strain of bacteria found, she was sent for a scan in February to check for abnormalities. All was clear.

The pain-free time was short lived. The tummy pains soon returned. Rebekah was referred to a pediatrician, but the waiting lists were extremely long. Having a health policy with Benenden, I requested an urgent appointment with a pediatrician of their choice, and in April 2018 Rebekah was seen by a pediatrician in Belfast. Blood tests were done which ruled out celiac and allergies. The pediatrician felt that Rebekah's bowel was causing her problems and prescribed Mebeverine medicine.

This medicine gave some, but not total, relief. In September Rebekah moved into Primary 3 and I became her teacher. Seeing her in school all day made me more aware of the persistent pain and discomfort Rebekah was experiencing. We persevered with the medicine, but as Rebekah was still not pain free our GP changed the medicine to Dicycloverine. Again this seemed to provide some relief, but with a very unpleasant taste, which Rebekah found difficult to take.

Rebekah would awaken from sleep regularly and complain of hunger. I gave her biscuits to stem the hunger and get her back to sleep, concluding that hunger and wind were two main contributors to the problem. Unknown to me at that time, the biscuits were contributing to the problem, as they contained wheat.

At that point conversations began with Darren, our pharmacist, around intolerances. Darren explained how an intolerance differs from an allergy in that, with an allergy you will see a quick reaction, whereas with an intolerance the reaction is delayed. The reaction can come between three and seventy-two hours later, which makes it more difficult to establish exactly what foods are contributing to the patient's pain and discomfort. I noted that Rebekah was in significantly more pain after eating Weetabix or ice cream. My friend Libby often commented that she felt Rebekah was reacting to some food as she herself suffers from IBS and food intolerances.

Becoming more convinced that we were dealing with intolerances, I decided to get an intolerance test done. As these tests are expensive, Darren encouraged me to only go down that route as a last resort, but after a year of struggles and no definite answers, we had indeed reached that point.

CHAPTER 3

Food Intolerances

A food intolerance occurs when a person has difficulty digesting a particular food. This can lead to many symptoms such as intestinal gas, abdominal pain, diarrhea or constipation.

The Mayo clinic states that "a true food allergy causes an immune system reaction that affects numerous organs in the body. An allergic food reaction can be severe or life-threatening. In contrast, food intolerance symptoms are generally less serious and often limited to digestive problems."[2]

A food intolerance test seemed to be the way to go. The York Intolerance test was recommended, and so we asked Darren if he could guide us down this route.

---

[2] James TC Li, M.D., Ph. D., "What's the difference between a food intolerance and a food allergy," Mayo Clinic, April 03, 2020, www.Mayoclinic.org/diseases-conditions/food-allergy/expert-answers/food-allergy/faq20058538

Rebekah was tested at the end of December 2018. It was done using a pin prick test, which was distressing for a young child, but we needed to know if Rebekah really was suffering from a food intolerance. Christmas was a good time to be tested as there is a variety of food on offer at this time of year and this is an advantage when it comes to intolerance testing. Darren's prediction was that numerous foods would show up. As we awaited the results, we did not realise how true his prediction would be...

The results came back at the beginning of January. Darren met with us and shared the results.

By that stage I guessed that gluten and lactose were the culprits, given Rebekah's previous reactions to Weetabix and ice cream. Preempting the results, I had introduced lactose-free butter, milk, and cheese and was beginning to look at gluten free bread.

The results showed that Rebekah had tested positive for intolerance to dairy (both cow and goat's milk), wheat, eggs, millet, and crustacean mix. Darren expected a shocked reaction but I was, naively, very calm. I had already introduced lactose-free food and we didn't eat a lot of eggs, so I wasn't particularly concerned. As for crustacean mix—well we didn't eat prawns or sea food of any description.

Darren explained that the normal procedure is to eliminate the problem foods for twelve weeks and reintroduce these foods gradually, one at a time. Twelve weeks seemed a long time, but I marked it out on the calendar. By summer it would be done and dusted, problem solved...

If only!

The truth began to hit home.

Dairy didn't mean *lactose*. It meant anything with milk protein. As we read food packages I soon discovered that there was milk in so many unexpected places, such as cheese-and-onion crisps. Being dairy free was a lot more involved than being lactose free. I had to consider changing to dairy free milk, butter, cheese, and ice cream. Cheese sauce had almost become a staple part of the diet. It was part of Sunday dinner and pasta dishes. Try making cheese sauce with dairy-free alternatives and the result is far from edible. The packet "free from" version could be made up using water. It was a slight improvement, but again ended up in the bin. This was a crisis! Life without cheese sauce? How could it be done? Only time would tell.

I then moved onto wheat. This didn't just include bread, but also cereals, biscuits, cakes, burgers, sausages, and many brands of crisps. By avoiding both wheat and dairy, Rebekah's choice of crisps became limited to Walkers salt and vinegar and ready salted. With the advice to avoid crustacean mix, I also excluded prawn and cocktail crisps.

"No eggs" eliminated cakes, buns, and other treats.

Millet I was unsure about. The only place I found it was in a gluten and dairy free pizza! I have since found millet flour.

And so, life as Rebekah knew it changed overnight.

Going out to church functions, when supper was provided, meant she could no longer eat anything as there was wheat in all the sandwiches and buns, not to mention the butter or cream or eggs hiding about.

Ice cream could no longer be readily enjoyed. Her favourite ice cream, honeycomb, had been taken away. Dairy free vanilla and chocolate were the only alternatives. How did they even compare with her other favourite flavours, parma violet and bubble gum?

Kids love parties and party food. Rebekah was limited to chips and gluten free breaded chicken. It was so hard for her watching other kids eat the birthday cake and buns, knowing that if she joined in she would suffer later. Parents were so accommodating, though, and bought free-from alternatives to help her.

No one, however, could take away her frustrations and struggles. No one could take away how left out she was feeling. Only God knew.

God had opened doors to pediatricians and food intolerance testing. I needed God to open more doors to enable Rebekah to enjoy life to the full.

CHAPTER 4

The Journey Continues...

At home I was on my own journey. I was feeling frustrated at my inability to make everything right again for Rebekah and provide food that would allow her to live a more normal life and feel included again.

Rebekah could no longer eat bread, and most gluten free brands also contained eggs. The only available alternative was a loaf of 'free from' bread from Tesco, which was free from wheat, milk, and eggs.

I found Ben and Jerry's ice cream, which is dairy free; however, upon reading the label I found it is not *wheat* free.

Life had become very complicated. Rebekah's diet was very restricted and lacked calcium, so I supplemented her diet with chewable calcium tablets designed for kids.

Through conversations with Darren I concluded that Rebekah was suffering from leaky gut. This is a condition well documented in America but not recognized by the medical profession in the UK.

Leaky gut happens when the tight junctions that hold your intestinal wall together become loose. Think of your gut lining as a drawbridge; very tiny boats that are meant to get through the bridge do so without a problem. This is how vital nutrients from food are absorbed into the bloodstream. Certain lifestyle and environmental factors, however, will cause the drawbridge to open and allow bigger boats to cross into the bloodstream which aren't supposed to be there. Toxins, proteins and partially digested food particles that were never meant to pass through the drawbridge are able to get into the bloodstream.[3]

This is what is meant by "leaky gut." The result is pain and inflammation.

Your gut contains trillions of bacteria. They help to digest your food and play an important role in your well-being.

The mix of bacteria in your body is different from everyone else's. It is known as your *microbiota* or *microbiome*. It is determined by your mother's microbiota (the environment you were exposed to at birth) as well

---

[3] Amy Meyers MD, *The Autoimmune Solution Cookbook (New York, NY : HarperOne, 2018), 24*

as your diet and lifestyle, which all make yours completely unique. The bacteria in your body affect everything including your mood, your metabolism and even your immune system.[4]

Scientists have discovered a link between your gut and illnesses such as diabetes, heart disease, and inflammatory bowel diseases.

Restoring beneficial bacteria to reestablish a healthy balance of good bacteria is critical.

For this reason, I included probiotics in Rebekah's diet daily. The probiotics used were 'UDOs' capsules for kids. When choosing a probiotic, it is wise to seek the advice of a pharmacist. Unfortunately, probiotics are expensive, but a good probiotic is what we needed to do the job.

Probiotics are live bacteria. Prebiotics, on the other hand, are considered to act as a fertiliser for the good bacteria in the probiotics. There are a number of healthy prebiotic foods, e.g. garlic, onions, leeks, and bananas.

Prebiotics can also be found in the supplement, inulin.

---

[4] "What your gut bacteria say about you", *webMD*, accessed Oct 28, 2020, https://www.webmd.com/digestive-disorders/what-your-gut-bacteria-say-your-health#1

There are also other products recommended for gut healing, such as L-glutamine. This is an amino acid that helps your gut lining repair itself.

Collagen is also recommended to heal damaged cells and build new tissue. This can be bought in powder form or made using chicken bones. I have listed the recipe for bone broth in the recipe section. I added bone broth as stock in vegetable soup.

As we continued our journey the Lord continued to open up doors one by one.

I was introduced to the "Free From Fairy," Vicki Montague. Vicki is a scientist who has developed a website called www.freefromfairy.com. Through the website I learned that Vicki had developed her own gluten-free flour blend along with a number of recipes. This flour is a multipurpose flour.

In addition, Vicki has a number of online courses available which include adapting to a gluten-free diet.

Using Vicki's flour and one of her recipes I was able to successfully incorporate pancakes into Rebekah's diet. These weren't normal pancakes, but included flax seeds and ground almonds, adding nourishment to Rebekah's diet. (Recipe included in the Recipe section.)

This was an introduction to a new level of culinary skill which would lead me on a steep learning curve into new recipes and foods.

Around this time my sister, Vivienne, recommended the film *The Secret Ingredients Movie*. [5] It is a life changing film which I would highly recommend.

The film focuses on health issues various people were experiencing and how changing their diet by removing GMO foods and buying organic food had a huge impact on their lives. It also refers to glyphosate, which has been used as a herbicide to spray crops. (This will be dealt with more fully in a later chapter.)

Pesticides are widely used in food production and affect our bodies in ways we are largely unaware of. One thing we do know is that their affects are not positive.

I was given a voucher as a gift and decided to buy a bread maker, as I wanted to bake bread without additives and also with the goal in mind of making gluten-free bread. I researched various makes and opted for a Panasonic 2500 bread maker. After purchasing it I wondered if I had made a mistake. How would I use it? Would I be able to make bread from it? I put it away and went on holidays, deciding I would give it a go on my

---

[5] Jeffrey Smith & Amy Hart, "The Secret Ingredients Movie", accessed Oct 28,2020, www.secretingredientsmovie.com

return. I didn't realise that it was a gift from God which would prove to be invaluable in the months ahead.

In August I decided, with trepidation, to finally use the bread maker. My anxieties turned to surprise as I produced my first loaf! It was baked using 'strong flour,' specially designed for baking. I baked a few more loaves and decided to try gluten-free bread. Gluten-free bread was different; the texture and taste did not compare to normal bread. My bread making began to incorporate organic flours according to what I had learned from *The Secret Ingredients Movie*.

As time progressed, I decided to try giving Rebekah "normal" bread using organic flour, which her body seemed to tolerate. She was able to enjoy honey and sunflower seed bread which was made using organic wholemeal bread flour and organic strong white flour with honey and sunflower seeds to flavour. This unfortunately was not long lasting due to the wheat. I changed to spelt flour and Rebekah experienced no reaction.

I then progressed to adding a slight skim of butter on her bread. Again, no reaction.

Libby, whom I mentioned previously, suffers from IBS and is also gluten- and dairy-free. She explained that she can eat cheddar cheese with no reaction, whereas other cheese causes her pain.

I tried giving Rebekah cheddar cheese, a little at a time, with no perceived reaction.

I wondered why cheddar cheese caused fewer digestive problems. I only recently discovered that cheddar cheese and butter are both permitted on the FODMAP diet[6]. The diet originated in Australia and has been adapted for the UK by researchers at King's College, London. FODMAPs are different carbohydrates found in a wide range of foods including onions, garlic, mushrooms, apples, lentils, rye, and milk. These sugars are poorly absorbed and pass through the small intestine and enter the colon where they are fermented by bacteria. Gas is then produced which stretches the sensitive bowel, causing bloating, wind, and pain.[7]

This diet seeks to eliminate any food which causes pain and discomfort in digestion. Libby explained that she can eat a Milk Tray sweet and a small Crunchie bar, which led me to try a Milk Tray with Rebekah and she was able to tolerate it. She has also enjoyed a Crunchie bar since then. Success! Libby has also found that she can tolerate Cadbury chocolate in small quantities but not Nestle! Why? That remains a mystery! I read an interesting article outlining how Cadbury's chocolate

---

[6] App: FODMAP A to Z, Developer Temaire 1798 Ltd

[7] Emer Delaney, "What is a low FODMAP diet?", BBC good food, updated Aug , 2018, https://www.bbcgoodfood.com/howto/guide/what-low-fodmap-diet

differs from other chocolate and tastes different in other countries, but it still does not explain why some people can tolerate this chocolate over others.[8]

As we moved into Autumn 2019 I discovered A2 milk in Tesco. Milk is made of two proteins: A1 and A2. The protein A1 causes most problems in people with digestive problems, whereas A2 is found to be better tolerated.

Rebekah was able to drink A2 milk without a reaction. It tasted like milk and contained all the nourishment of milk because it was, after all, milk! I will deal more fully with A2 milk later.

A2 milk was another breakthrough in terms of cooking for Rebekah. It meant that I could once again give Rebekah cheese sauce, using milk, butter and cheddar cheese. That was a great day for Rebekah, having cheese sauce once again with her Sunday dinner. She savoured the taste that day with a wide smile on her face. It was such a blessing watching Rebekah once again enjoy cheese sauce. This was the breakthrough another friend, Stephanie, had prayed for, that God would provide cheese sauce for Rebekah. Initially it had seemed impossible, but we had seen God's guidance and provision to get to that place.

---

[8] Elle Metz, "Does Cadbury Chocolate Taste Different in Different Countries", BBC News, March 18,2015, https://www.bbc.co.uk/news/magazine-31924912

Again, I felt the Lord had led me to make this discovery. Darren was the only other person I knew who had ever heard of A2 milk. Unfortunately this joy was short lived, as A2 milk soon disappeared from our supermarket shelves. The A2 company, which is based in New Zealand, had withdrawn from the UK due to lack of sales. I was saddened by this but not shocked, as the milk had never been promoted.

I tried pancakes with a milk substitute but Rebekah no longer enjoyed the taste, after having tasted them with "real" milk. She sobbed at breakfast time, the pancakes ended in the bin, and we all went to school distressed.

Tesco was able to find and reserve the last remaining cartons of A2 milk in another store, which I promptly froze to ensure it would last as long as possible! God was good. It reminded me of how much He cares for every detail in our lives. He cared that a little girl needed pancakes for her breakfast and provided what she needed.

I searched for more A2 milk but to no avail. I needed to source it somehow. This led me to Natonic in Australia[9]. This company sells powdered A2 milk in one liter bags. Each bag can make seven liters of milk.

God was faithful. Bread, cheese, and milk had now been restored to Rebekah's diet.

---

[9] "*Natonic*," 2018, www.natonic.com.au,

As the journey continued through Christmas, Rebekah tried gluten-free stuffing from the butcher. This left her in a lot of pain, as there was butter and eggs in the recipe. This confirmed to me the difference homemade cooking was making. But I now needed to make stuffing for Rebekah. I tried my mum's recipe, but used my own bread made from spelt flour. It was a success and is now a standard part of Sunday dinners.

CHAPTER 5

Back to the Beginning?

As we fast forward to March 2020, the old problems seemed to resurge. Rebekah's sore tummy flared up and she had persistent pain. I tried removing gluten but had no success. In early June I made an appointment with the GP. By that stage I was questioning how much the anxiety of coronavirus was contributing, yet Rebekah's tummy was also bloated.

The GP decided to use Movicol, having considered that constipation may be an issue. Still, the sore tummy persisted. A stool test ruled out anything serious but the mystery of what was causing it remained. Rebekah had an appointment with a pediatrician in early July where an x-ray confirmed an overloading of the bowel, and so the use of Movicol was increased. This helped greatly. However, when considering Rebekah's symptoms (gas, bloating, constipation, nausea, abdominal pain) it appears to link in with IBS, especially as this is often triggered by stress. As there is no test to prove this I can only assume that this is a possibility.

Through the time of coronavirus, I used the opportunity to research new recipes for Rebekah. We made a new chocolate cake, which I may add didn't last long! I tried making yogurt, too, as fermented food is said to be good for gut healing. I also tried bone broth. Unfortunately the taste of natural yogurt was not a hit, so this developed into homemade ice cream following the gift of an ice cream maker. The children claim this is the best way to eat yogurt!

I persisted with the yogurt making and found a recipe which also included vanilla and honey. This transformed our yogurt making, and made homemade yogurt a regular part of our family's diet. This ensures that good bacteria are included regularly in Rebekah's diet.

As time passed the pain in Rebekah's tummy subsided—only to be replaced by nausea. This was still ongoing when she started back to school in September. On a few occasions the nausea was so severe Rebekah could only lie down and wait until it passed.

A further appointment with the pediatrician was scheduled for September 2020. At this appointment it was decided that Rebekah would be given Sanomigran at night and double the Movicol intake.

As I write this, we are now at the end of October 2020, and I am thankful that the nausea is subsiding. Rebekah is currently feeling better than she has done for months. She is still taking her medication and I monitor her diet closely.

I look at Rebekah, a child who has faced the huge challenge of intolerances, and feel glad that we have worked through it together as a team. It has been a difficult time for Rebekah—a time of both physical and emotional pain—yet she has persevered. She has been willing to try new food but longs to be able to eat freely like other children.

My prayers are that the Lord will heal her totally so that she will not be restricted by what she eats. It has been a slow journey but we have come a long way. Often we pray and expect an immediate answer from the Lord. Yes, He can heal and has healed people instantly and miraculously, but I have learned that some healing takes place over a period of time. We need to keep praying and trusting in the Lord each step of the way, knowing He loves us and holds us in His hands. He will never fail us, but will walk with us each step of the way.

I have learned new culinary skills and learned a lot about intolerances. I appreciate all those who have taken the time to support us and pray for us along the way. The Lord has been faithful. He has opened doors and provided. If you are walking through your own journey, I pray that you too would know the Lord's faithfulness and goodness as you face your challenges.

> *"The LORD is faithful to all his promises and loving toward all he has made." (Psalm 145:13)*

CHAPTER 6

What is glyphosate?

Many I'm sure will be wondering what glyphosate is. Glyphosate is a herbicide which is used to kill weeds such as annual broadleaf weeds and grasses that compete with crops.

Glyphosate is rarely used on its own, but as part of a chemical cocktail. One of these cocktails can be found under the trade name Roundup.

Dr. Robin Mesnage of King's College London writes, "We know Roundup, the commercial name of glyphosate herbicides, contains many other chemicals, which when mixed together are 1,000 times more toxic that glyphosate on its own." [10]

---

[10] Robin Mesnage, "Monsanto loses court case concerning the safety of glyphosate", *garden organic,* Aug 13 2018, www.gardenorganic.co.uk

The World Health Organisation claims that glyphosate may be carcinogenic (meaning it could contribute to or cause cancer) and can also affect kidneys and liver.

Monsanto is the company which produces Roundup. In 2018 Dewayne Johnson, a forty-six year old former groundskeeper, was the first person to take Monsanto to trial. The jury supported his claim that Roundup weed killer caused his cancer and the corporation failed to warn him of the health hazards from exposure. He was awarded $78 million in damages.[11]

As of 2020, Monsanto have had to pay a further $10 billion to settle cancer suits. The parent company, Bayer, faced tens of thousands of claims linking the weed killer to cases of non-Hodgkin's lymphoma. Some of this money has been set aside for future cases.[12]

Glyphosate is not just used in the US, but in many countries across the world. Despite concern, the UK have extended its use until 2022![13]

---

[11] Emily Sullivan, "Groundskeeper Accepts Reduced $78 Million Award in Monsanto Cancer Suit," NPR, Nov 1, 2018, www.npr.or

[12] Alex Formuzis, "Bayer-Monsanto Agrees to $10B Settlement With Victims Poisoned by Roundup Weedkiller, ewg, Jun 24, 2020, www.ewg.org

[13] "Status of Glysophate in the EU", European Commission, accessed Oct 28, 2020, www.ec.europa.eu

In addition to glyphosate, Monsanto has also been involved in producing genetically modified crops (GMOs) which have been altered to make them more resistant to certain pests, diseases, or environmental conditions. Examples of genetically modified crops in the US include soybeans, corn, canola, wheat, and potatoes.

There have been many debates about the safety and risks of GMOs. Many believe that GMO foods can have harmful effects on the human body. By consuming them it is believed that they can also cause the development of diseases which are immune to antibiotics.

No GM crops are grown commercially in Britain. However, animals are often fed GM crops. Meat, milk, and eggs fed with GM crops are eaten by people in the UK. In the UK, organic milk and eggs are available, however, which means that the milk, for example, comes from cows which have not been fed GM crops.

CHAPTER 7

Organic vs Non-Organic

There are a number of advantages to buying organic produce:

1) No GMOs used
2) No synthetic pesticides linked to lymphoma and leukemia
3) No Roundup herbicides, which are linked to kidney disease, breast cancer, and birth defects
4) No growth-promoting antibiotics contributing to weight gain and antibiotic resistance
5) Organic foods prohibit many of the chemicals known as "obesogens" that trigger our bodies to store fat

A recent study showed that organic produce is richer in nutrients and antioxidants and lower in heavy metals and pesticides.[14] Other studies suggest that good soil

---

[14] Lauren Morello, "Study finds Organic Produce is more Nutritious," news-blog, Jul 11, 2014, www.blogs.nature.com

nutrition increases the production of cancer-fighting compounds called flavonoids, while pesticides and herbicides disturb their production.[15]

It is advisable to buy organic oats as regular oats contain pesticides including glyphosate. Bear in mind that oats are found in many products which are deemed healthy, like cereal and cereal bars.

There are a number of organic products available in local supermarkets, but this varies from shop to shop.

---

[15] Amy Meyers, "3 Reasons to Eat Organic if you have an Autoimmune Disease," *Amy Meyers MD*, updated Aug 26, 2020, www.https://www.amymyersmd.com/article/eat-organic-autoimmune/

CHAPTER 8

How Wheat Has Changed...

For thousands of years, grain has always been at the heart of mankind's diet. Nowadays we find many have turned to gluten-free breads due to intolerances and digestive issues. The underlying problem is that modern wheat is making people sick. What has caused this?

The world's wheat was transformed in the 1950s and 60s in a movement called the "Green Revolution." This involved initiatives to develop high-yielding varieties of cereal grains. This movement was pioneered by Norman Borlaug. He developed a new and "improved" species of semi-dwarf wheat which, with fertilisers and pesticides, yielded great crops of wheat, to the detriment of future generations' health. The wheat we now know is only a distant relative of the wheat once grown just forty years ago.[16]

Scientists are now realising there is a connection between modern wheat and the many chronic digestive and inflammatory illnesses people face today.

I read the following quote, which in my mind sums up our modern wheat.

> *"We have mutant seeds, grown in synthetic soil, bathed in chemicals. They've deconstructed, pulverised it to fine dust, bleached and chemically treated to create a barren industrial filter that no creature on this planet will eat. And we wonder why it is making us sick?"*[17]

Some people suffer from celiac disease, which means that they can be negatively affected by the slightest trace of gluten. However, many others are affected not so much by the *gluten*, but by modern wheat. Thus there is a difference between being gluten intolerant and being sensitive to modern wheat.

---

[16] The Editors of Encyclopaedia Britannica, "Norman Ernest Borlaug," *Britannica*, Updated Sep 8, 2020, https://www.britannica.com/biography/Norman-Borlaug

[17] "What's wrong with modern wheat", *Grainstorm Heritage Baking*, accessed Oct 27, 2020, https://grainstorm.com/pages/modern-wheat

With Rebekah I have tried to minimise gluten as far as possible, as bread seems to have triggered reaction, but I believe that Rebekah is one of those suffering from sensitivity to modern wheat rather than to gluten. The results of her intolerance test signified an intolerance to wheat but not gluten, which would support this theory.

Heritage Flours

Compared to modern wheat, heritage grains have a lower gluten content and are healthier and easier to digest. This is the case with einkorn flour, for example. Einkorn is one of the earliest cultivated varieties of wheat.

There are a lot more health benefits associated with heritage grains. They provide a larger array of vitamins and minerals, and have up to forty percent more protein than regular wheat and up to sixty-five percent more amino acids.[18]

Shipton Mill, in England, produces heritage flour, milled from 150 varieties of heritage flour.[19]

---

[18] "Why Heritage Flour", The Heritage Flour Baking Co., Accessed Oct 28,2020, https://www.heritageflourbaking.com/pages/why-heritage-grains

[19] "Heritage Flour," Shipton Mill, Accessed Oct 28, 2020, https://www.shipton-mill.com/flour-direct-shop/flour/heritage-flour

Spelt Flour

I use spelt when making bread and pizzas. I also purchase spelt spaghetti and other pastas. There are a number of benefits from using spelt flour, the main reason being it is easier to digest. I have found that Rebekah can tolerate food made with spelt flour.

It has been claimed that the fiber and other nutrients in spelt and other whole grains can help to improve the health of the good bacteria that live in your digestive system. It may help to reduce inflammation and promote healthy digestion.[20]

Organic v Regular Wheat Flour

Organic flour is milled from pesticide-free grain and grown in soil only fertilized by natural substances. It's also been said that organic grain develops more robustly, taking in more nutrients from the soil and thereby making the flour healthier and more nutritious.

Also, if it is not organic or labelled *unbleached*, then your white flour has been bleached. Bleached flours have had all their germ and bran content removed.

---

[20] "Spelt- is it good for you?" Nourish, Accessed Oct 29, 2020 , https://www.webmd.com/diet/spelt-good-for-you

CHAPTER 9

2020 Dirty Dozen Foods

Each year a list is compiled of the top twelve foods containing the most pesticides. Buying organic versions of the list (where possible) should help reduce risks associated with pesticides.

Strawberries, kale, and spinach were at the top of the list last year.

1) Strawberries
2) Spinach
3) Kale
4) Nectarines
5) Apples
6) Grapes
7) Peaches
8) Cherries
9) Pears
10) Tomatoes
11) Celery

12) Potatoes

Tip: Washing fruit and vegetables with 2% salt water will remove most of the contact pesticide residues that normally appear on the surface of the vegetables and fruits. I regularly do this with strawberries as they can be hard to source organically. It also removes any bugs or dirt lurking on the outside of strawberries!

CHAPTER 10

2020 Clean Fifteen Foods

In contrast to the dirty dozen, the Environmental Working Group have also produced a list of the fifteen foods with least pesticides. [21]

1) Avocados
2) Sweet corn
3) Pineapple
4) Onions
5) Papaya
6) Sweet peas (frozen)
7) Eggplants
8) Asparagus
9) Cauliflower
10) Cantaloupes
11) Broccoli
12) Mushrooms
13) Cabbage

---

[21] Pamela Riemenschneider, "Dirty Dozen, Clean Fifteen lists updated for 2020," Blubook Services, March 25,2020,

14) Honeydew melon
15) Kiwi

Before moving on, it is worth spending a few minutes looking a bit deeper into these foods.

1) Avocado
Out of a batch of 360 avocados, fewer than 1% had pesticide residues; of those with residues, only one type of pesticide was found.

2) Sweetcorn
Less than 2% of sampled sweetcorn, including corn on the cob, had detectable pesticide residues. However, this list doesn't include the residues of glyphosate. Also worth bearing in mind is that the majority of starchy field corn used in processed foods is from genetically modified seeds. Organic corn is not genetically modified nor sprayed with glyphosate, but is unfortunately hard to source.

3) Pineapple
90% had no detectable pesticide residues due to their thick skin. It is worth noting that pesticides from pineapple plantations in Costa Rica have contaminated drinking water and killed fish. Organic may be worth buying, though again is hard to source.

4) Onion

Pesticides were detected on less than 10% of sampled onions. Organic onions can be up to 20% higher in flavanols, which are compounds which protect heart health.

Keeping raw onions in the room when you are sick is a folk remedy that dates back to the 1500s. During the bubonic plague, onions were placed around homes to keep people from contracting the deadly illness.

There is conflicting evidence that leaving a cut onion in a room will protect again illness. Having said that, I found a couple of online quotes:

"Please remember it is dangerous to cut an onion and try to cook it the next day. It becomes highly poisonous for even a single night and creates toxic bacteria which may cause adverse stomach infections because of the excess bile secretions and even food poisoning." [22]

"Onions are a huge magnet for bacteria, especially uncooked onions. You should never plan to keep a portion of sliced onion. It's not even safe if you put it in a zip-lock bag and put it in your refrigerator." [23]

---

[22] Jenny McCoy, "Are Cut, Raw Onions Poisonous," Explore Cooking Light, March 28, 2018, https://www.cookinglight.com/eating-smart/nutrition-101/are-cut-raw-onions-fridge-poisonous

[23] Snopes Staff, "Cut Onions Contamination Warning," Snopes, Feb 16, 2009, https://www.snopes.com/fact-check/cut-onions-contamination/

I will finish these thoughts on onions with a story from 1919.

In 1919, when the flu killed 40 million people, there was this doctor that visited the many farmers to see if he could help them combat the flu. Many of the farmers and their families had contracted it and many died.

The doctor came upon this one farmer and to his surprise, everyone was very healthy. When the doctor asked what the farmer was doing differently, his wife replied that she had placed an unpeeled onion in a dish in each room of the house (probably only two rooms back then)

The doctor couldn't believe it and asked if he could have one of the onions and place it under a microscope. When the doctor placed it under a microscope he found the flu virus in the onion! [24]

I'll leave you to reach your own conclusion!

5) Papaya
Around 80% of avocados tested had no detectable pesticide residues. The majority of Hawaiian papayas, however, have been genetically modified to resist a virus that can destroy the crop. Organic is therefore a better choice.

---

[24] David Emery, "Can Raw Onions Absorb the Flu?" Liveaboutdotcom, Sep 28, 2018, https://www.liveabout.com/raw-onions-and-flu-3299608

6) Frozen Sweet Peas
Around 80% had no detectable pesticide residues. The pod is exposed to pesticides and appears to shield the peas.

7) Eggplants / Aubergines
Close to 75% analysed were free of pesticide residues.

8) Asparagus
About 90% tested had no detectable pesticides. Asparagus contains an enzyme which helps break down Malathon. Malathon is a pesticide commonly used against beetles that attack the vegetable. This may explain why asparagus is featured in the clean fifteen.

9) Cauliflower
Although in the clean fifteen, only 50% of cauliflowers were found to have no detectable pesticide residues. The pesticide imidacloprid was found on 30% of samples. This pesticide has been linked to declining honeybee and bumblebee populations. In my opinion, cauliflower is a vegetable where organic is a preferable choice.

10) Cantaloupes
Over 60% of those tested had no detectable pesticide residue. The interesting fact about this fruit is that harmful bacteria may contaminate the rind and transfer to the flesh when you cut it. Advice is that you should scrub cantaloupe and other melons with a clean

brush and cool tap water before cutting. Melons can cause food poisoning and should always be refrigerated when cut, to reduce this risk.

11) Broccoli
Of the samples taken, about 70% had no detectable pesticide residues. Like cabbage, it contains glucosinolates, which act as insect deterring plant compounds. Again, like cabbage it is also rich in plant compounds which reduce inflammation and help protect one from cancer.

12) Mushrooms
One of the vegetables with least pesticides. They are rich in B vitamins, magnesium, potassium, selenium, and fiber.

13) Cabbage
Cabbage produces glucosinolates, which deter harmful insects and therefore needs less spraying. Glucosinolates may help prevent cancer.

14) Honeydew Melon
Around 50% contained no detectable pesticides. This is a fruit which I have yet to source as organic. Remember the advice given in the cantaloupe section regarding cut melons.

15) Kiwi

You may be unaware of the fact that the skin of a kiwi is indeed edible and is also a good source of fibre. 65% of those tested had no detectable pesticides. I find it concerning that in those tested with residue, up to six different pesticides were noted.

It may be worth considering organic kiwi, as these are easy to source.[25]

To conclude, these are the fruits and vegetables least affected by pesticides not including glyphosate, but it is always worth considering organic versions where available.

---

[25] Marsha McCulloch, "The Clean Fiftieen, Foods that are low in pesticides," *Healthline,* Oct 24, 2018, https://www.healthline.com/nutrition/clean-15

CHAPTER 11

A2 Milk

A2 milk is a milk which few have heard about. The questions I am frequently asked are: What is it? How does it differ from regular milk?

Regular milk contains both A1 and A2 beta-casein proteins, but A2 milk contains only A2 beta-casein. It is currently produced in Australia, America, Guernsey, and Mainland UK.

Interest began to grow in the distinction between these two proteins in the 1990s. Scientists in New Zealand found that there was a link between the prevalence of milk with A1 beta-casein in some countries and the prevalence of chronic diseases.[26]

---

[26] Atli Arnarson,"Adverse Claims about A1 Milk," Healthline, March 14,2019, https://www.healthline.com/nutrition/a1-vs-a2-milk

African and Asian cattle produce only the A2 beta-casein, whereas the A1 beta-casein is common among cattle in the Western world. [27]

When the A1 protein is digested into the small intestine it produces a peptide called BCM-7. Symptoms of stomach discomfort such as gas, bloating, and diarrhea that occur after consuming dairy products are typically attributed to lactose intolerance. Some researchers believe that it is the peptide BCM-7 from the A1 protein which is causing the symptoms.[28]

A study was carried out in 2016 as to the effects of drinking regular milk, during which some effects became evident.[29]

1) There were higher levels of inflammatory markers after drinking regular milk.
2) Brain function was affected. After drinking milk with the A1 protein, it took longer for a person to process information compared to drinking

---

[27] "History", *Wikipedia A2 milk*, updated Oct 27,2020, https://en.wikipedia.org/wiki/A2_milk

[28] Atili Arnarson, "Digestive Health,"

[29] Nutr J. 2016; 15: 35. Published online 2016 Apr 2. doi: 10.1186/s12937-016-0147-z

A2 milk. Fewer errors were made by those who drank A2 milk.[30]

3) Some animal studies have shown associations between cow's milk consumption and a higher incidence of type 1 diabetes. One study in mice found that 47% of the mice that had the A1 protein added to their diet developed diabetes. Other research does not support the link. [31]

Many people throughout the world, who previously could not drink milk, can now enjoy A2 milk. It tastes the same as regular milk. It is the same without the A1 protein. If milk is causing you digestive problems, it would be worth checking out A2 milk. You may be able to enjoy all the nutritional benefits of drinking milk without the after affects.

Unfortunately, since the milk company withdrew from the UK, it has not been available in Northern Ireland.

The good news is that Ian Patterson and his son Thomas James, who own Parklands Dairy Farm in County Down are planning to launch sales of this milk in the near future.

---

[30] Megan Metropulos, MS, RDN, "The Benefits and Risks of A2 Milk," *Medical News Today*, July 25, 2017, https://www.medicalnewstoday.com/articles/318577

[31] Katie, "Importance of A2 Milk", Millhorn Farmstead, Aug 19, 2019, https://rawsomedairy.com/importanceofa2milk

They can be contacted on 00447801526657.

CHAPTER 12

E Numbers

E numbers are codes for substances used as food additives for use within the European Union. They are commonly found on food labels, but I have become increasingly concerned about side effects from these additives.

A couple of years ago we were in Spain and the children found ice pops you could buy in the supermarket and freeze later.

I noticed that every time they ate one of these ice pops their behaviour totally changed. They became hyperactive and "silly." They didn't appear to be able to control their behaviour. On closer inspection, I found the ingredients contained lots of E numbers.

As I researched these additives further I found that a number of them can cause hyperactivity in children and some others are carcinogenic.

Many colours, which are added to food to make it more attractive and appealing, contain E numbers which give cause for concern.

It may surprise you to know that "Sunset Yellow" food colouring (E110) can be found on children's painkillers. This colouring should be avoided by anyone with asthma, rhinitis, or urticaria (hives)!

Below is a table containing the most dangerous E numbers [32]

Name	E Number	Where found	What you should know
Allura Red AC	E129	Food coloring in snacks, sauces, preserves, soups, wine, cider	Avoid if you have asthma, hay fever, or hives
Amaranth	E123	Food color in wine, spirits, fish roe	Avoid if you have asthma, hay fever, hives, or allergies. Banned in US
Aspartame	E951	Sweetener in drinks, snacks etc	Possibility of headaches, blindness or seizures with long term, high doses
Benzoic Acid	E210	In drinks, low sugar products, cereals & meat products	Avoid if you have hay fever, hives, or asthma

---

[32] "What are the most dangerous e-numbers," accessed Oct 28, 2020, https://talkingaboutthescience.com/studies/E-numbers.pdf

Brilliant Black BN	E151	Drinks, sauces, snacks, cheeses etc	Avoid if you have asthma, rhinitis, hives etc
Butylated Hydroxyanisole (BHA)	E320	Preservative in fat containing foods, confectionary, meats	Can possibly cause cancer. Reacts with nitrates to form chemicals which cause change in DNA cells
Calcium Benzoate	E213	Preservative in drinks, low sugar products, cereals, meat products	Avoid if you have hay fever, hives, asthma
Calcium Sulphate	E226	Preservative in foods from burgers to biscuits	Can cause bronchial problems, flushing, low blood pressure, anaphylactic shock
Monosodium Glutamate (MSG)	E621	Flavor enhancer	Can cause pressure on head, seizures, chest pains, headaches, nausea, etc.
Ponceau4R, Cochineal Red A	E124	Coloring	Worsens symptoms of asthma, rhinitis or hives
Potassium Benzoate	E212	Preservative in drinks, low sugar products, cereals, meat products	May deplete amino acid levels. Avoid if have hay fever, hives or asthma

Potassium Nitrate	E249	Preservative in cured meats (e.g. bacon) and canned meats *Nak'd bacon is free from nitrates & is now available in Tesco*	Can lower oxygen carrying capacity of blood, can combine with other substances to create nitrosamines which can cause cancer
Propyl P-hydroxy-benzoate, Propylparaben, Paraben	E216	Preservative in Pates, cereals, snacks, meat products & confectionary	Identified as cause of chronic dermatitis
Saccharin and its Na, K and Ca salts	E954	Sweetener found in diet and no added sugar products	It has been concluded that this may cause cancer
Sodium Metabisulphite	E223	Preservative & antioxidant	May provoke life threatening asthma
Sodium Sulphite	E221	Preservative in wine making and other food processes	Can trigger asthma attacks
Stannous Chloride (tin)	E512	Antioxidant & color retention agent in canned and boiled foods & fruit juices	Causes nausea, vomiting, diarrhea, and headaches
Sulphur Dioxide	E220	Very widely used preservative	Avoid if you suffer from conjunctivitis, bronchitis, emphysema, bronchial asthma or cardiovascular disease
Sunset yellow FCF, Orange – Yellow S	E110	Widely used food color	People with asthma, rhinitis or hives should avoid

| Tartrazine | E102 | Widely used yellow food color | May cause allergic reaction in 15% of population. Can cause asthmatic attacks and hyperactivity in children. May cause symptoms of asthma, rhinitis & hives to worsen |

It is worth noting that E102, E122, E129, E104, E151 & E133 have already been banned in a number of countries, including Austria and Norway.[33]

Other websites worth investigating are:

www.exploreenumbers.co.uk
www.curezone.org/foods/enumbers.asp

---

[33] "What are the most dangerous e numbers?" accessed Oct 29, 2020, https://talkingaboutthescience.com/studies/E-numbers.pdf

CHAPTER 13

Digestive Enzymes

Your body makes enzymes in the digestive system, including the mouth, stomach, pancreas, and small intestine.

Naturally occurring digestive enzymes are a vital part of your digestive system. Without them your body can't break foods down so that the nutrients can be fully absorbed.

Certain health conditions can interfere with the production of digestive enzymes. When that is the case, you can supplement digestive enzymes before meals to help your body process food effectively.

Digestive enzyme supplements take the place of natural enzymes, helping to break down carbohydrates, fats and proteins.

Taking a supplement of digestive enzymes can be of benefit in gastrointestinal disorders. Because they are meant to mimic your natural enzymes, they must be taken just before you eat. That way, they can do their work as food hits your stomach and small intestine. If you don't take them with food they won't be of much use.[34]

Rebekah has found this supplement to be beneficial in helping her digest food. It gives immediate results.

---

[34] Ann Pietrangulo, "The Role of Digestive Enzymes in Gastrointestinal Disorders," *Healthline*, Feb 28,2020, https://www.healthline.com/health/exocrine-pancreatic-insufficiency/the-role-of-digestive-enzymes-in-gi-disorders

CHAPTER 14

Recipes

I would recommend the following websites for gluten-free recipes. I will refer to any recipes that I particularly liked. I try to choose recipes without too many ingredients and which are both simple to make and, of course, tasty! I tend to cook in larger quantities when I find a recipe I like and freeze for future meals.

1) www.glutenfreepalate.com
2) www.freefromfairy.com
3) www.glutenfreerecipebox.com (this website will be closing in August 2020 so I will print some recipes I would recommend)
4) www.bbcgoodfood.com (not gluten-free, but recipes can be adapted)

BREAD

A lot of my bread is made in a bread maker. I use a Panasonic 2500, which can be purchased in Argos. I would highly recommend this bread maker. However, if you plan to buy a bread maker you may wish to consider the 2501 model, which is available on Amazon. Model 2501 is more expensive but more recipes can be set on a timer.

The bread maker comes complete with a recipe book, which is invaluable. My favourite breads are granary and honey & sunflower seed. I have substituted spelt flour in the honey and sunflower recipe for Rebekah. I also use the white spelt bread for stuffing. Using a bread machine is very simple. Simply add the ingredients in the order listed and turn on! Most breads contain yeast, white/ wholemeal flour, sugar, salt, butter, and water. Compare that to the ingredients on store bought bread. The one disadvantage is that homemade bread can take a few minutes to prepare but three to five hours to knead, rise and bake. But the results are worth it!

Tip: When storing 1kg bags of flour, I find the storage boxes from Tesco useful. It is also useful to cut the label off the flour, with the flour's name, as well as the expiry date. These labels can then be attached to the storage box.

I have used Allinson Easy Bake Yeast in breadmaking and find it works well. During the lockdown yeast was scarce and I sourced it through eBay. There are a few sellers who sell Fermipan Red, but price varies.

Amazon sells clear storage containers specifically sized for bread made in bread makers. Bread can be sliced and frozen in containers. Larger loaves need to be placed horizontally in storage box when sliced.

GLUTEN-FREE BREAD

I find gluten-free breads are generally less palatable, but I found two recipes which I would recommend.

This recipe is designed for a bread maker. [35]

---

[35] "Panasonic Automatic Breadmaker. Operating Instructions and Recipes. Model No. SD-2501/SD-2500" Taiwan 2011

Ingredients

3200ml water
1 tsp cider vinegar
4 tbsp vegetable oil
1 medium egg
1 medium sized egg white
450g gluten-free white bread flour mix
1 tbsp sugar
1 tsp salt
2 tsp yeast

Put into bread maker in correct order and set to gluten-free setting.

I used apple cider vinegar and olive oil. Doves Farm Gluten Free Bread Mix is recommended. I used Shipton Mill's and was pleased with result. Another gluten-free bread recipe can be found on www.glutenfreepalate.com This is a lovely bread and quite sweet. It can be baked with or without a bread maker.

PANCAKES

Gluten-free / dairy free / egg free

Ingredients

1 egg / equivalent using Orgran Egg Replacer
1 tsp organic milled flaxseed (Linwoods)
1 tsp baking powder
Approx. 20-30g organic ground almonds
Approx. 80g gluten free flour
Dairy free milk /equivalent

Method

1) Whisk egg/mix egg replacer with correct amount of water
2) Add flaxseed and baking powder and stir

3) Add ground almonds and flour and mix
4) Add enough milk to create a batter which is not too runny nor too thick.
5) Fry on pan at a low heat. Turn when batter is bubbling on top.

Tip: I use a gluten-free flour blend from the Free From Fairy website (www.freefromfairy.com). It is a wholemeal blend and will transform your pancakes! As I don't add sugar, Rebekah enjoys her pancakes with a dairy free chocolate spread.

REGULAR PANCAKES

I regularly cook pancakes for my other children which are not gluten- or dairy free.

Ingredients

1 egg
Approx. 150g self-raising flour
1 tsp flaxseed (optional)
Milk
Choice of spread

Method

1) Whisk egg
2) Add flour and flaxseed
3) Add milk and mix until batter is fairly thick
4) Add to a preheated pan. Tilt pan to spread batter more thinly as mixture will rise
5) When bubbles form, turn over
6) Leave for short time until other side is cooked
7) Remove from pan and cover with a tea towel
8) As there is no sugar in the mixture, honey or chocolate spread are good options to spread on pancakes!

Tip: I have tried so many different flours for pancakes but the best is Shipton Mill's organic self-raising flour. The pancakes are extremely light and fluffy with this flour and have been voted tops by Rachael and Caleb!

STUFFING

I use white spelt bread, made in the bread maker, as a base. White spelt does have gluten, but it has a different molecular make up than modern wheat and is easier to digest. Spelt is also higher in fiber than wheat, and the extra fiber aids in the digestion of the gluten. As it has gluten proteins, it *should* promote inflammation but it doesn't.

Always remember spelt may be a good alternative for some but is unsuitable for those with celiac disease or gluten sensitivity.

Ingredients

Spelt breadcrumbs
Fresh parsley
Onion
Butter/dairy free alternative
(I use organic onion and organic unsalted butter, both from Tesco)

Method

1) Using a food processor, add parsley and onion to breadcrumbs
2) Add a good-sized knob of softened butter to bind
3) Wrap stuffing in tinfoil. Cook at 200 for approx. 30 mins. Open tinfoil for 5 mins if stuffing is not browned

Stuffing can also be frozen if not needing to cook immediately.

HOMEMADE CHICKEN GOUJONS

Ingredients

Gluten free flour
Egg/ milk
Breadcrumbs/ stuffing
4 chicken breasts, sliced

Method

1) Place each ingredient in a separate dish.
2) Grease 2 baking trays
3) Dip each chicken piece in flour, then egg/milk, then breadcrumbs and place on tray

4) When all chicken is coated cook at 200 for approx. 25-30 minutes.

Tip: I find the breadcrumbs stick better when using egg. If using stuffing instead of breadcrumbs you will have more flavour.

My children love these!

CHEESE SAUCE[36]

This is a very versatile sauce. I add it to pasta, potatoes, chicken dishes, etc.

The recipe is for one portion. I would tend to multiply the recipe, depending on requirements

Ingredients

½ oz butter
1 tablespoon flour (gluten free if required)
6 fl oz milk (or dairy free)
1 ½ oz cheese

Method

1) Melt the butter in a saucepan
2) Remove from heat and stir in flour
3) Add milk and bring to the boil
4) Remove from heat and stir in cheese

---

[36] Annabel Karmel, "New Complete Baby and Toddler Meal Planner," Ebury Press, London, 2011

CHICKEN, LEEK, BACON & CHEESE SAUCE

Ingredients

4 breasts of chicken diced
1 leek
2 slices of bacon
Cheese sauce (see recipe)
Paprika (optional)
Salt
pepper
Quantities can be adjusted to taste.

Method

1) Fry chicken until tender
2) In another pan fry chopped bacon and leek until soft.
3) Cook amount of cheese sauce required depending on how much sauce you would like
4) Drain the chicken. Add leek and bacon.
5) Pour cheese sauce over and mix
6) Add paprika, salt & pepper to taste

SPELT PIZZA[37]

Ingredients

1 cup warm water
Approx. 3-4 cups white spelt flour
2 ¼ tsp active yeast
2 tbsp coconut sugar
1 ¼ tsp salt
1 tbsp olive oil (or similar)
Tomato puree
Grated cheese

---

[37] Sarah, "Easy spelt Flour Pizza Dough," Making thyme for health, Oct 4, 2017, https://www.makingthymeforhealth.com/easy-spelt-flour-pizza-dough/

Method

1) Heat water in microwave until quite warm but not hot
2) Put water into mixing bowl
3) Sprinkle yeast over
4) Sprinkle coconut sugar (will activate yeast)
5) Leave for 10 mins. Mixture will look frothy
6) Add oil, salt, 1 cup flour and mix together
7) Add 2 cups flour and mix
8) Add flour gradually until dough is not too sticky.
9) Put dough in a large greased bowl and put in a warm oven that has been turned off.
10) Leave for 45 mins-1 hour to prove (rise)
11) Cover pizza trays with baking paper. Roll dough into 2 large pizzas.
12) Spread tomato puree onto base
13) Sprinkle grated cheese
14) Cook in oven at 200°C or 400°F for approx. 10-12 mins

Tips:

1) 1 cup of white spelt flour can be substituted for 1 cup wholemeal spelt flour (my children prefer this!)
2) Use some flour when working with the dough to prevent it sticking to hands / rolling pin!
3) Roll dough onto baking paper first. When approx. correct size place baking paper onto tray and use a knife to shape pizza.

4) Napolina double concentrated tomato puree works well

VEGETABLE SOUP

Those who are gluten-free will be unable to tolerate the barley in this recipe. I included it as soup mix containing barley, lentils, etc. gave Rebekah a sore tummy. When I tried the organic soup mix from www.buywholefood-sonline, Rebekah was able to eat the soup without any after effects!

I have only recently started cooking this in a slow cooker. I save and freeze the stock from cooked chicken and use at least a pint in this recipe.

Soup mix needs to be soaked for a few hours beforehand.

Ingredients

Approx. 300g soup mix (adjust to suit)
3 packets of soup vegetables
3 chicken stock cubes
At least 1 pint chicken stock

Method

1) Place soup mix in slow cooker and cover with boiling water
2) Cook for two hours on high
3) Add vegetables & hot chicken stock
4) Use boiling water and chicken stock cubes to make up additional stock
5) Cook on high for two to three hours or until vegetables are soft.

MANGO CHICKEN

Ingredients

1 packet sweet peppers
1 container mushrooms
6 chicken breasts diced
2 onions
Mango chutney
1 ½ pts chicken stock
Natural yogurt (optional)

Method

1) Fry onions and chicken until chicken fairly well cooked
2) Add sliced peppers and mushrooms
3) Cook until chicken and vegetables are cooked.
4) Add to an oven proof casserole dish
5) Add mango chutney (either small jar or half large jar) & stir in
6) Pour over chicken stock
7) Cover with tinfoil and place in oven at 200 for approx. an hour
8) If desired natural yogurt can be stirred in to make casserole creamy and lessen the sharp taste. If not eating immediately, leave the casserole to cool before adding yogurt.

Tip: adjust quantities of vegetables and chicken to suit taste and quantity required. Mango chutney can be increased if a sweeter casserole is required.

BONE BROTH[38]

I came across this recipe in *The Autoimmune Solution Cookbook* by Dr Amy Myers.

Preparation time is short, but cooking time is 24-48 hours. I added bone broth to my vegetable soup as it is renowned for its healing properties and collagen content.

Many people drink a mug daily to gain full benefit.

Ingredients

1 organic/free-range leftover chicken carcass
2 tbsp apple cider vinegar
1 tsp fine sea salt
2 garlic cloves (peeled and smashed on flat side with a knife
1 cup of carrots/celery/onions
8 cups filtered water (or as needed)

Method

1) Put chicken in slow cooker with vinegar, salt, garlic, and vegetables.

---

[38] Amy Meyers MD, *The Autoimmune Solution Cookbook (New York, NY : HarperOne, 2018), 71*

2) Add enough water to cover bones
3) Set slow cooker to low and cook for 8-24 hours. (the longer you cook, the more collagen/gelatin you extract from bones)
4) Remove bones and sieve broth
5) Refrigerate for 4 days or freeze for up to 2 months

SPAGHETTI BOLOGNESE[39]

400g tomatoes can be used. I chose cartons of organic tomatoes, as the resin linings of tin cans contain BPA. This has been linked to ailments ranging from reproductive problems to heart disease and obesity. The acidity from tomatoes can cause the BPA to leak into your food.

Ingredients

500g mince
1-2 onions
1 tsp rosemary
1 tsp oregano

---

[39] www.bbcgoodfood.com

1 tsp basil
2 bay leaves
2x 390ml cartons organic chopped tomatoes
1 beef stock cube

Method

1) Fry onions & rosemary for 2-3 mins
2) Add mince
3) When brown add chopped tomatoes, oregano, basil & bay leaves
4) Crush stock cube and mix in
5) Bring to a boil and simmer until cooked through. Give time for flavours to soak through.

If time allows I cook this in a slow cooker.

The following recipes can be found on www.glutenfreepalate.com

1) **Gluten-free chocolate cake** – I substituted regular milk for coconut milk and it worked well. Please note that prior to putting into the oven it will be in a liquid state, resembling hot chocolate! It will turn into a solid cake as it cooks.

2) **Chocolate cake donuts** – tasty but more like cake than donuts. They didn't last long with my children!

3) **Gluten-free Bread** — I mentioned this in a previous section

4) **Gluten-free flour blend** — this is recommended for use in these recipes. It is easy to make and ingredients can be sourced at www.buywholefoodsonline.com

2 cups white rice flour
1 cup tapioca starch
1 cup potato starch

Mix ingredients well together and store in an airtight container.

The following recipes can be found on www.bbcgoodfood.com

1) **Easy chicken tagine** – this has a tang of ginger and sweetness of honey. Great served with potatoes, rice or even pasta.

2) **Chicken, sweet potato, and coconut curry** – This is a delicious mild curry. I use probably half recommended curry paste as we do not eat very spicy food. The recipe produces a lot of sauce. You could half the amount of sauce and increase amount of chicken and sweet potato.

I serve with rice but Rachael enjoys it with a thick slice of homemade granary bread. I**MAGE 16**

3) **Chicken Korma** – if you like chicken korma then this is a great recipe. I omitted the sultanas.

4) **Chicken Biryani –** I reduced the curry paste to 1 tbsp and it was spicy enough!

The following recipes can be found on www.freefromfairy.com

1) **Creamy butternut squash soup**

2) **Veggie burgers –** with oats and nuts

3) **Oven baked chicken & bacon casserole**

Wraps

I have tried different recipes for wraps/flatbread but the most successful has been with spelt flour and can be found on www.ohsheglows.com

Recipes in all websites are regularly updated

CHAPTER 15

Yogurt Making

This has been a recent venture, as I read that fermented foods were source of healing for the gut (unless you are following a FODMAP diet).

Yogurt making can be viewed as time consuming. However, it is similar to bread making in that the preparation time is short but it takes time for the machine to do the job.

I have been using a LUVELE Yogurt maker.[40] If you consider making yogurt, I would recommend this model. There is also excellent customer support.

Basic yogurt making involves heating milk to 82 degrees and holding the milk at that temperature for 10 minutes if possible. Cool milk down to 42 degrees when the yogurt starter is added. (A thermometer is required for

---

[40] www.luvele.co.uk

this. Thermometers can be found on Amazon. Check it can be clipped onto saucepan for best results.)

The starter is mixed into the milk and the mixture added to the special yogurt container. This is placed in the machine to ferment for twelve hours. Some people find the natural yogurt quite tart. LUVELE has developed a recipe where vanilla and honey are added, which creates a much milder taste.

LUVELE has demonstration videos on YouTube.

CHAPTER 16

Ice Cream!

Needless to say, this has been the best food I have made to date, as far as Rachael, Rebekah, and Caleb are concerned!

www.biggerbolderbaking.com is a website which has recipes where an ice cream machine is not required.

I started this venture as I was given a machine as a gift and it provided a means for Rebekah to enjoy honeycomb ice cream again!! Having said that, her current favourite is now lemon!

Ice cream is not difficult to make. www.bbcgoodfood.com have a recipe for honeycomb ice cream with tips if you do not have an ice cream maker.

This website also has a recipe for honeycomb, which tastes much better than shop bought; I have tried both!

CHOCOLATE ICE CREAM [41]

I am going to include a recipe for chocolate ice cream. I use A2 milk, dairy free chocolate, and Elmea Plant cream.

Ingredients

225ml full fat milk
100g granulated sugar
200g milk chocolate broken into 1cm pieces
450ml double cream
1tsp vanilla extract

Method

1) Heat the milk, cream, and vanilla in a medium pan over a medium heat until just bubbling around the edges.
2) Place sugar and chocolate into a food processor and process until finely chopped.
3) Add hot milk to food processor and mix until smooth.
4) Transfer to a medium bowl to cool completely. Cover and refrigerate for at least 2 hours, preferably overnight
5) Churn ice cream in ice cream maker

---

[41] Cuisinart, Ice cream & Gelato Professional ICE100BCU (instruction manual), 17

YOGURT AND RASPBERRY ICE CREAM [42]

For this recipe I use homemade yogurt, but shop bought yogurt will be fine.

Ingredients

125g raspberries
300ml plain yogurt, chilled
100g caster sugar

Method

1) Crush raspberries or blend in food processor. Sieve to remove the pips
2) Combine sugar and yogurt with the fruit puree
3) Churn in ice cream maker for 20-30 mins
4) Serve immediately or store in freezer in a suitable container.

---

[42] Magimix le Glacier 1.5 , *Libble.eu*, accessed Oct 28,2020https://www.libble.eu/magimix-le-glacier-1.5/download-387381/

CHAPTER 17

Products

There is wide range of 'Free From' foods available in our supermarkets. However, I have sourced food products from a variety of places to enable us to eat as much organic food as possible.

The following is a list of various suppliers I use. As far as suppliers of flour are concerned, it is also worth comparing the cost of shipping and flour, as it can vary considerably from company to company.

1) Natonic www.natonic.com.au
Suppliers of A2 milk. Sold in powdered form in 1kg bags. No more than 2kg may be imported to N. Ireland per shipment.

2) Shipton Mill www.shipton-mill.com
The mill has a wide range of flour available, both organic and non-organic. This includes gluten-free flours. My personal choices are organic white bread flour, organic

wholemeal bread flour, organic light malted, and organic spelt.

3) Doves Farm www.dovesfarm.co.uk
Another company which sells good quality organic flour. Some products may be available in local supermarkets. Gluten-free flour available.

4) BuyWholefoodsOnline www.buywholefoodsonline.co.uk
Organic flour is available, as well as organic pasta, coconut sugar, tapioca starch, potato starch, and organic dried fruits (e.g. dates, raisins).

5) Planet Organic www.planetorganic.com
As the name suggests it sells a wide range of organic products. This includes gluten-free pasta and spaghetti, which is made from organic corn and rice. It tastes just like regular pasta. This company also sells tinned coconut milk for baking which doesn't contain additives you find in the supermarket. Coconut oil, coconut sugar, coconut condensed milk, and cream are also available. They also sell chewing gum without additives—a bit pricey but it tastes good!

6) Wholemeal flour blend www.freefromfairy.com
This flour is pricey but makes great pancakes. Can be used in other recipes but I find it changes taste.

Conclusion

As we reach the end of this part of the journey I hope you will have developed a fuller understanding of the role the food industry plays in our health, and have been guided to make better food choices.

But most of all I hope you have seen that despite how difficult and challenging the journey can be, we do not need to journey alone.

I hope you are already walking with the Lord, but if you are not, take time now to consider asking Him into your life. He loves you so much that He died on the cross for you. He gave up everything so that you could have a relationship with Him and one day be in heaven with Him forever.

We make decisions about food and many other issues daily, but the decision you make about whether or not to follow Jesus is the biggest and most important decision you will ever make. I trust you too will ask Him to forgive you and to come into your life. He does not want you to journey alone.

For further information about knowing Jesus or even if you have a question regarding what I have shared in this book, please contact me.

Blessings,
Heather

Bibliography

Meyers, Amy MD. *The Autoimmune Solution Cookbook.* New York, NY : HarperOne, 2018.

Lightning Source UK Ltd.
Milton Keynes UK
UKHW050744170522
403115UK00006B/108